EXTREME BITERS

BLACKBIRCH PRESS

An imprint of Thomson Gale, a part of The Thomson Corporation

THOMSON
———————✦———————™
GALE

Detroit • New York • San Francisco • San Diego • New Haven, Conn. • Waterville, Maine • London • Munich

THOMSON

GALE

Photo credits: Cover: bottom right, middle left © Discovery Communications, Inc.; top right © Royalty-Free/CORBIS; top center, bottom left © Digital Stock; top left © Digital Vision; middle right Corel Corporation; interior: all pages © Discovery Communications, Inc., except for pages 1, 36 © Digital Vision; page 4 © Photos.com; page 8 © Karen Tweedy-Holmes/CORBIS; pages 12, 20, 45 © Digital Stock; page 16 © A.N.T./Photo Researchers, Inc.; page 24 © Michael & Patricia Fogden/CORBIS; page 28 Corel Corporation; page 32 © Royalty-Free/CORBIS; page 40 © Gwen Lowe/SeaPics.com

LIBRARY OF CONGRESS CATALOGING-IN-PUBLICATION DATA

Biters / by Sherri Devaney, book editor.
 p. cm. — (Planet's most extreme)
 Includes bibliographical references and index.
 Summary: Explores ten animals with unusual biting abilities and compares these abilities to humans.
 ISBN 1-4103-0389-6 (hardcover : alk. paper) — ISBN 1-4103-0431-0 (pbk. : alk. paper)
 1. Bites and stings—Juvenile literature. 2. Mouth—Juvenile literature. 3. Anatomy, Comparative—Juvenile literature. I. Devaney, Sherri. II. Series.

 RD96.2.B55 2005
 617.1—dc22

                                                      2004021042

Printed in the United States of America
10 9 8 7 6 5 4 3 2 1

Some people bite off more than they can chew, but they are no match for the biggest and worst biters in the natural world. We're counting down the top ten most extreme biters in the animal kingdom, and comparing them to a dentist's worst nightmare! Stand by for the tooth, the whole tooth, and nothing but the tooth, when biting is taken to The Most Extreme!

10

The **Mosquito**

Flying into number ten is an animal that really gets under your skin. Meet the mosquito, the smallest and deadliest creature in the countdown. You can't escape from this flying bloodhound, because it tracks you down by following the minutest traces of carbon dioxide from your breath.

The mosquito is the mother of all biters because it's only the female mosquito that uses her amazing proboscis to suck blood. It's human blood that nourishes mosquito eggs, so that's why the female has the most complicated biting apparatus in the countdown. It's a combination of Swiss army knife, hypodermic needle, and vacuum cleaner! But once she's tapped into a blood vessel, the victim's problems have only just begun, for traveling in her saliva are some deadly hitchhikers.

That's why the mosquito is number ten in the countdown. Her bite can be lethal, but it took people some time to make the connection between certain forms of sickness and the mosquito.

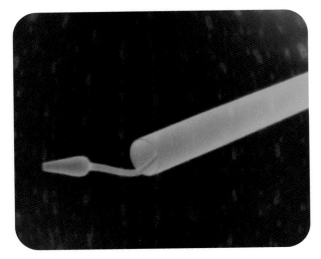

Under a microscope, you can see the female mosquito's proboscis is perfectly designed to tap into blood vessels and suck blood.

A hundred years ago the scourge of the American military was yellow fever, or yellow jack. An army doctor had a hunch the disease was spread by mosquitoes, but to prove it, he needed some human guinea pigs. Sure enough, once these unfortunate volunteers were

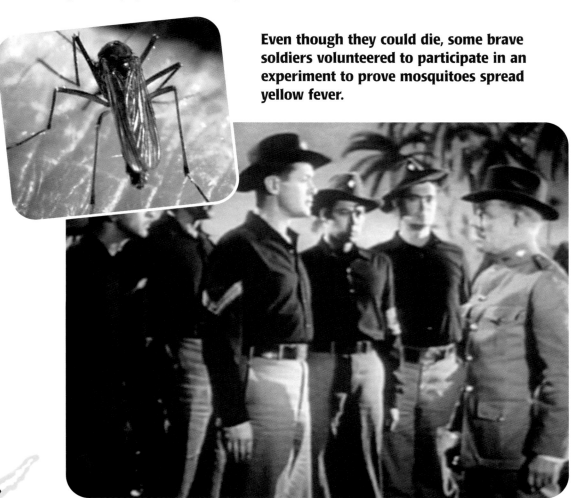

Even though they could die, some brave soldiers volunteered to participate in an experiment to prove mosquitoes spread yellow fever.

Mosquitoes spread many diseases through their bite, including malaria, which even today claims lives all over the world.

bitten, they picked up the parasite transmitted by mosquito spit. But yellow jack is only one of the diseases spread by the mosquito's deadly bite. The queen of the killers is malaria, a disease that causes high fevers and sometimes death. Even today, malaria spread by mosquitoes will kill one out of every seventeen people on Earth.

9

The Naked Mole Rat

The mosquito may be deadly, but its bite barely scratches the surface of the next contender in our extreme countdown. Meet the naked mole rat. It's a hairless rodent that spends its life beneath the plains of Africa, building tunnels with its teeth! It's number nine in the countdown because it has a jaw-dropping mass of muscle.

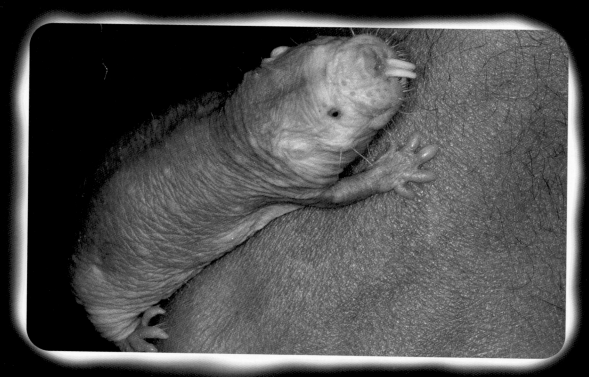

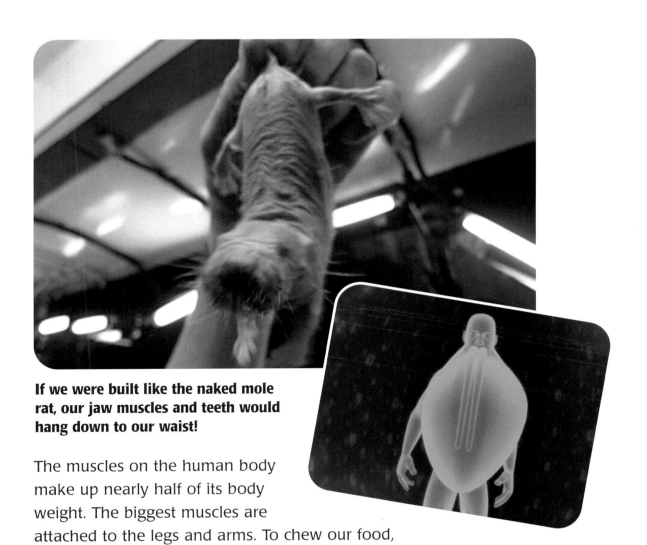

If we were built like the naked mole rat, our jaw muscles and teeth would hang down to our waist!

The muscles on the human body make up nearly half of its body weight. The biggest muscles are attached to the legs and arms. To chew our food, we move our jaw using only about 1 percent of our muscle mass. But imagine if humans were like the naked mole rat! If we spent our lives tunneling with our teeth, our jaw muscles would make up a quarter of our muscle mass!

These bucktoothed beauties are an orthodontist's nightmare. Naked mole rat moms don't lose any sleep over their offsprings' overbite, however. Only humans do, which is why an estimated 5 million Americans of all ages are braced for better teeth.

The only thing the naked mole rat is braced for is action! He has concrete reasons for liking his teeth just the way they are.

Millions of people wear braces for a prettier smile, but you'd never find a mole rat complaining about its buckteeth.

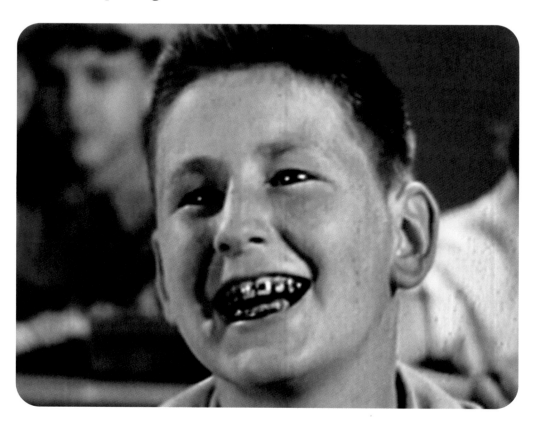

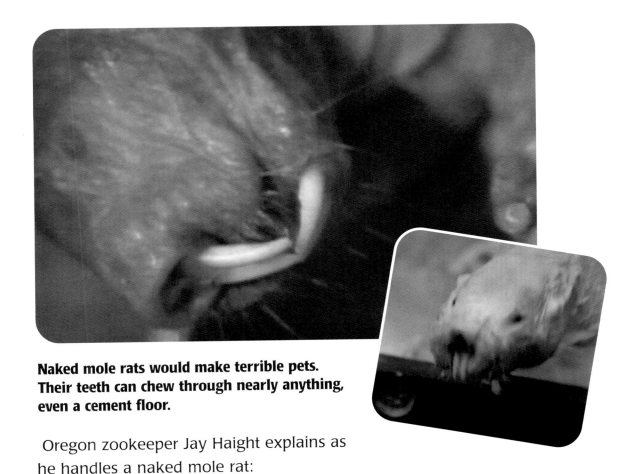

Naked mole rats would make terrible pets. Their teeth can chew through nearly anything, even a cement floor.

Oregon zookeeper Jay Haight explains as he handles a naked mole rat:

> If I were to drop him right now, given enough time he'd actually chew through the cement of the floor down here. These chambers are specially constructed with acrylic and then some steel mesh and then some material known as hydrostone. The object here is to keep them from chewing through the hydrostone into the steel mesh because then you have a nightmare of chamber repair. They're a little on the feisty side.

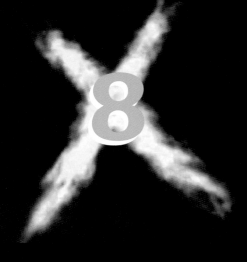

The Snake

Slithering into number eight in our countdown of extreme biters is the snake. Every year more than 7,000 Americans have close encounters of the venomous kind, and on average fifteen of these will be fatal.

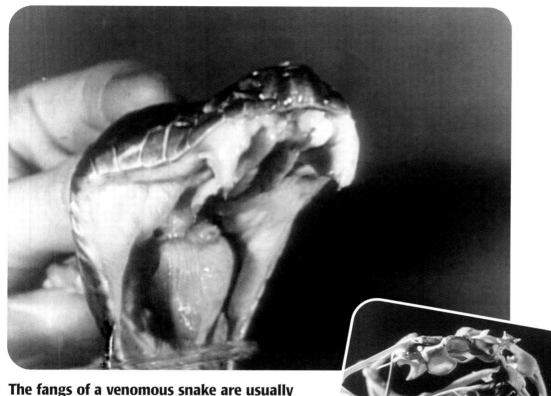

The fangs of a venomous snake are usually nestled against the roof of its mouth, but they swing forward when the snake strikes (inset).

People die of snakebites because venomous snakes inject their poisons with teeth shaped like hypodermic needles. When a snake isn't using its fangs, they are folded back against the roof of its mouth. When the snake strikes, the fangs swing forward. Imagine these hypodermic needles penetrating several inches into the skin before the snake venom is injected. This deadly bite allows the snake to deliver its poison deeper into the wound of its victim.

The Australian outback is home to the worst biters of all. Snakes are number eight in the countdown because the bite of an inland taipan delivers enough potent venom to kill half a million mice or 100 people. Even baby taipans are lethal!

Adult taipans have enough venom to kill half a million mice. This little guy wants to be like dad, but he's starting out with just one mouse.

Don't be fooled by this baby taipan's size! One bite from this pip-squeak could easily kill you!

Although only 10 percent of snakes are venomous, it pays to stay well clear of any animal that bites first and asks questions later. Without venom, even a human's best bite can't match the horror of a snakebite. No wonder snakes strike fear into people around the world.

The Funnel Web Spider

Sydney, Australia, is home to the next contender in our countdown of extreme biters. Crawling into number seven is the funnel web spider. The funnel web spider strikes like lightning, and the enormous fangs inject paralyzing venom deep into its prey. These fangs are even strong enough to drive through a lizard's skull, but they are no use when it comes to eating. That's why funnel web spiders have a different way of digesting their dinner.

Imagine if we ate like a funnel web spider. A pair of fangs would be great for killing food, but useless for chewing. So we'd have to make ourselves a little liquid lunch. Funnel web spiders throw up special enzymes that turn their meal into a soup that's simply sucked up.

The problem is that funnel web spiders don't eat fresh prey, and don't always stay out in the garden. The funnel web is one of the world's most dangerous spiders. It can sink its fangs through your fingernail and inject a poison that can be lethal, especially for children.

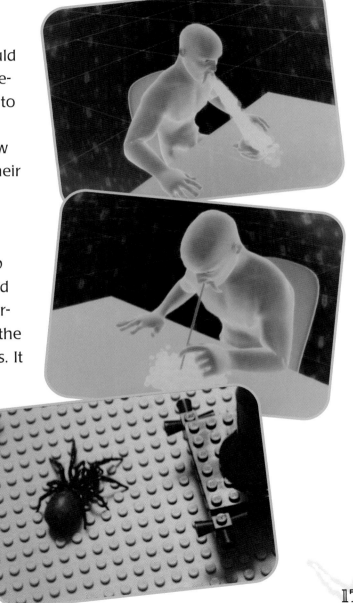

Would you want to eat like a funnel web spider? If you had fangs, you'd have to spit up all over your food and suck up the soupy mess.

In the last eighty years, funnel web spiders have killed more than a dozen people. But at the Australian Reptile Park, some spiders are helping to save lives.

Mary Rayner has one of the most extreme jobs on Earth. She milks killer spiders. Funnel web spiders are so aggressive that when they are provoked, venom drips from their fangs. All you need is a steady hand and nerves of steel to suck up the poison into a glass straw.

Mary Rayner uses a glass straw to retrieve the venom that drips from the fangs of a funnel web spider.

The funnel web spider's fangs are large and powerful enough to penetrate a child's fingernail.

The venom then gets used in the manufacture of an antidote to the spider's deadly bite. At least the funnel web spider no longer has our fate in its fangs, unlike our next contender.

19

The **Crocodile**

Life on the plains of Africa is as hectic as any city sidewalk. But this crosswalk is patrolled by a cold-blooded killer, and jaywalkers don't stand a chance. The crocodile is number six in the countdown because its jaws slam shut like a steel trap. Powered by enormous muscles, the crocodile's bite strength has been estimated at 3,000 pounds per square inch. That's more than ten times stronger than the average human bite!

A crocodile attacks a zebra, driving its sharp teeth into the animal.

That means all 60 of the crocodile's cone-shaped teeth are driven into flesh with the force of a sledgehammer. Once a crocodile has its teeth in you, it's almost impossible to escape.

Some people would like to have a bite as strong as a crocodile's! One group called the ironjaw rollerskaters have pulled everything from planes to ocean liners with their mouths. Even a crocodile would be proud of pulling a 320-ton ship a record-breaking 20 feet!

But most crocodiles have smaller fish to fry. A lineup of these massive jaws and teeth is a terrifying sight because more than just fish are on the menu. Any living thing that enters the water is a potential meal.

Gripping a chain in his strong jaws, a member of the ironjaw rollerskaters pulls a plane and tows a 320-ton ship.

Forget the enemy! Many Japanese soldiers in Myanmar during World War II died trying to wade through crocodile-infested swamps!

In waters around the world, each year crocodiles claim an estimated 2,000 lives. Crocodiles can hold their breath for up to an hour, which means they can swim right into the shallows in front of you. When a crocodile attacks, there's usually no warning, and you'll never know what got you.

Crocodiles even fought in World War II. The British in Myanmar had the Japanese army surrounded on an island. One thousand men tried to escape through croc-infested swamps. After the crocodiles attacked, only twenty men made it out alive!

5

e Bat

No one is safe f ... untdown of
extreme biters. ... ally do exist,
which is why th ... er five in the
countdown. Fall ... erica and you're
instantly on the ...

Numbed by anesthetic from the vampire bat's saliva, this sleeping seal doesn't feel a thing as a hungry bat feeds on its blood.

The tricky part is getting the blood without waking the victim. That's why these extreme biters have a numbing anesthetic in their saliva. Wouldn't it be great to have the bat's painkilling spit next time you're at the dentist?

The vampire bat doesn't have to worry about the dentist because it has fewer teeth than any other bat! These bats don't need to chew their food because they have a specially grooved tongue to lap up their bloody meal. The day after the bat has eaten there is little evidence that it has been feeding. If only Dracula were as subtle—but then he's not the only one with a distinctive bite.

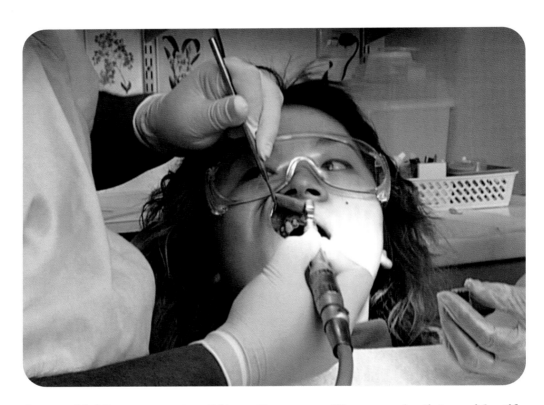

Open wide! Because no two bite patterns are alike, your dentist can identify you just by taking a peek in your mouth!

Dentists can easily identify patients because humans' 32 teeth leave a bite that is as unique as a fingerprint. That means people involved in forensic dentistry can catch criminals and identify bodies.

For centuries people have been polishing these forensic skills. During the Revolutionary War an American general by the name of Joseph Warren was killed at Bunker Hill, and his body was buried in an unmarked grave. A year later, it was decided to dig him up for a proper burial. The search for the dead general came to a dead end, however, because no one could tell the various bodies apart. Finally, a Boston dentist named Paul Revere identified the fallen hero by his distinctive dental work. The world's first forensic dentist was already famous, however. He galloped into the pages of history by taking a wild ride across the Massachusetts countryside to alert his fellow colonists that British troops were approaching.

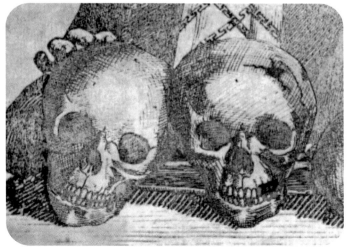

A dentist by trade, Paul Revere identified a Revolutionary War general buried in an unmarked grave by examining his teeth.

4

The **Dog**

Although vampire bats are also famous, they are not very loved because these extreme biters will sink their teeth into any large mammal they can. One animal in the countdown people generally do love is the dog. You can find a dog in more than one-third of all American homes. Today in the United States alone, the dog population exceeds 50 million. But man's best friend has a dark side.

The dog may be our best friend, but those sharp teeth can really hurt! Dog bites injure millions of Americans every year.

Dogs are number four in the countdown because, sometimes, their bite is much, much worse than their bark. Each year dogs bite more than 4.7 million Americans. Domestic dogs are now found in so many homes that you have a 1 in 50 chance of being bitten by a dog each year! And sometimes those bites can be deadly. In the United States alone, it's estimated that dogs will kill more people than those who die as a result of bites from grizzlies, alligators, and spiders combined!

Even the most extreme biters can get help at a veterinary practice in Manhattan Beach, California. This is because veterinary dentist Dr. David Neilsen has found a way to take the bite out of some canine criminals. Dr. Neilsen explains:

> Here at my practice we deal with dogs that have a bad reputation as a biter. Dog trainers classify a bite as one in which blood is drawn. A dog trainer will tell you that if a dog has bitten that hard

David Neilsen takes the bite out of a dog's teeth by filing down its powerful canines.

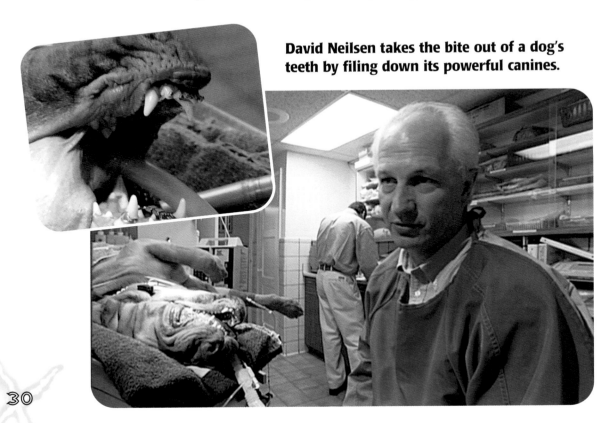

This friendly pooch thinks shaking hands is the best way to live up to his reputation as man's best friend.

they can't be trained to not bite. It's like asking a person to never get angry again, it's impossible. And so what we'll do is take off the canines, which are the fangs, at a certain level, halfway below the level of the incisors. After such a procedure the dog goes from being a biter to being a pincher. Not surprisingly it changes the dog psychologically. All of a sudden the dog is much more mellow. We've done this on a number of dogs and without problems afterwards, so it is kind of a neat way to save their lives.

Thanks to Dr. Neilsen, now even The Most Extreme biters can dream of being man's (and woman's) best friend.

31

3

The Komodo Dragon

Moviemakers imagined big scary reptiles and man-eating monsters, but Hollywood didn't have to invent these giant reptiles because one loathsome lizard already exists. Falling into number three in the countdown is the Komodo dragon. This extreme biter looks like it's from a long time ago.

On remote islands of Indonesia, these giant lizards reign supreme. Komodo dragons are number three in the countdown because just one bite is all it takes to bring down an animal the size of a buffalo. To make things worse, this dragon has the world's worst halitosis. Inside its mouth, festering meat trapped in the Komodo's teeth turns its saliva into a bacterial broth. Just one bite is enough to cause a fatal infection.

Komodo dragons have more than 60 teeth, and all of them are as sharp and serrated as steak knives. Its teeth are almost as deadly as the bacteria in its septic saliva. But then human mouths are also full of bacteria.

Because the Komodo dragon feeds on rotting meat (below), its saliva is filled with millions of deadly bacteria.

The bacteria in a human mouth may not be deadly, but they do cause tooth decay. Tooth decay is the most common disease in the world. A person's teeth are under attack by billions of bacteria that grow in a layer called plaque. When we eat sugary foods, so do the bacteria. They turn the sugars to acids, and acids eat into tooth enamel. But the human body can fight back. Our spit is full of minerals that replace the ones dissolved away by plaque acids. Each day a person produces about a quart of saliva. This means in your lifetime, you make enough saliva to fill a swimming pool, and that's more than 6,500 gallons of spit!

In a lifetime, the average human produces nearly 6,600 gallons of bacteria-fighting spit. That's enough to fill a swimming pool!

6600
GALLONS

Americans really love to chew gum. They go through millions of sticks a day!

Chewing gum is a great way to get the saliva glands pumping. But as well as fighting bacteria, chewing's been shown to relieve tension. So it's no wonder that during World War II soldiers chewed six times more gum than civilians!

Even now Americans chew their way through more than 50 million sticks of gum every day! Komodo dragons and their diseased drool have no need for bubble gum, but even their mighty mouth is no match for our next contender.

The **Hippopotamus**

In Kenya, the peaceful pond is home to the hippopotamus. They look so graceful that it's hard to imagine why hippos should be number two in the countdown. But making eye contact with a hippo could be the last thing you ever do. The hippopotamus is number two in the countdown because any trespasser will quickly learn that it's one murderous mammal.

No, these male hippos aren't kissing. Their jaws are locked as each tries to bite the other with his razor-sharp canines.

At the Honolulu Zoo, keeper Mary Rosolowich knows exactly how dangerous hippos can be. She explains:

> *Hippos kill more people in the wild than any other animal, including really dangerous ones like lions, tigers, and bears. This is because hippos are very territorial. Although they don't eat people, they do chew them up. A hippopotamus can open its jaws to 150 degrees. The males' lower canines are razor sharp and can grow up to twenty inches long. The hippos can even kill each other with a single bite.*

A male hippo has a mouth that opens more than 4 feet wide. It's this extreme bite that puts the hippo in at number two in the countdown.

A big mouth comes in handy when it's time for a dental checkup. Not that hippos need much more than a quick fish floss. Their teeth are so strong they inspired the earliest dentists. There was a time when false teeth were crafted from hippo ivory. In fact, it was a hippopotamus that gave George Washington his ring of confidence.

False teeth were once made from hippo ivory, including the fake pearly whites worn by George Washington.

Porcelain teeth were an improvement, but they still didn't have the same shine as natural teeth. So in 1942 dentists mixed in uranium to add a real glow, and to fill the mouth with more than four times the normal level of radiation.

Uranium stopped being added to false teeth in the 1980s, to the relief of the 32 million Americans whose teeth go out at night. And even though they're number two in our countdown of extreme biters, it will be a relief to most hippos to know their teeth don't end up in the mouth of a president.

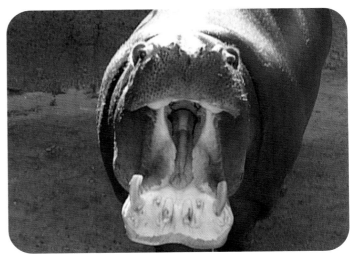

These days, false teeth are made from porcelain. That's good news to this hippo showing off his pretty teeth.

The **Cookie-Cutter Shark**

The most extreme biting animal in the countdown lives in the sea. The number one most extreme biter in the countdown, the cookie-cutter shark, earned its place because in the 1970s it forced a nuclear submarine to return to base. Something had attacked the layer of neoprene rubber covering the sensitive sonar dome in the bow.

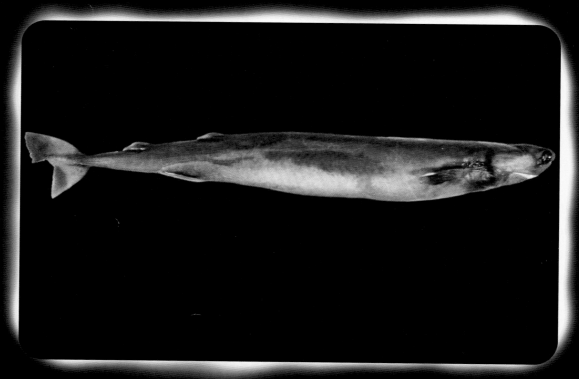

Careful study showed that the submarine had been hit by something that removed a perfect plug of rubber, 2 inches wide and 2½ inches deep. It looked like the attacker had just come straight from the kitchen! The plugs in the neoprene rubber looked as though they had been sliced by a cookie cutter. And that's just what happened.

The teeth responsible for the attack belonged to the cookie-cutter shark. For its size, the cookie-cutter has the largest teeth of any shark in the sea. But it doesn't normally eat submarines.

Although the cookie-cutter shark is a tiny fellow, its jaws are strong enough to tear into a nuclear submarine.

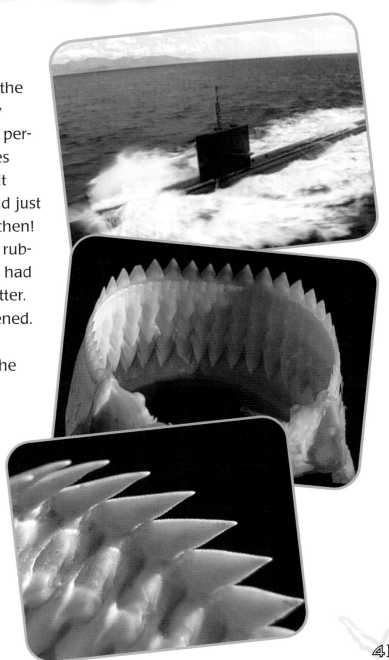

41

If you're not a dentist, pulling teeth is no easy job. Our 32 teeth are meant to stay put in our gums and last a lifetime.

Sharks are constantly replacing old teeth with newer, sharper versions. Wouldn't it be nice if humans weren't quite so attached to their teeth? Then pulling teeth wouldn't be such a giant job. All 32 adult teeth are firmly anchored in our jaws. Our teeth are meant to last us a lifetime, but then we don't put as much strain on our teeth as a shark.

The average human bite strength is only about 300 pounds per square inch. Compare that to a shark. Their jaws are estimated to generate forces 100 times more power- ful. And they go through teeth like nothing on Earth. In its life- time, a shark can go through 20,000 of these disposable steak knives! But for its size, the cookie-cutter shark has the largest teeth of any shark in the sea. We'd go through a few teeth as well if our bite strength topped the scales at 40,000 pounds per square inch!

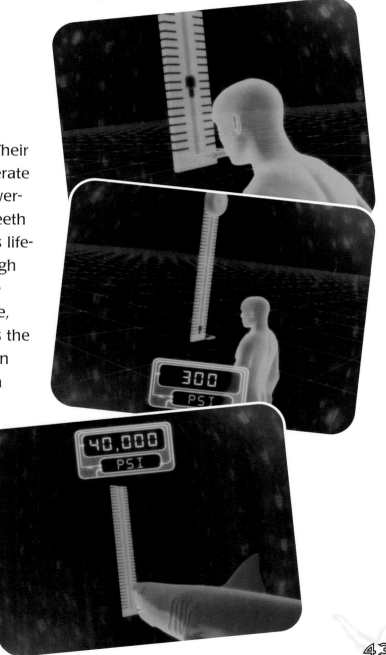

Compared with the strength of a shark's bite, the bite of a human is barely strong enough to chew gum.

43

Like the great white shark, the cookie-cutter shark is always on the lookout for something to sink its teeth into. Nobody's ever filmed what goes on far beneath the waves, but scientists know that the cookie-cutter shark, one of the smallest sharks in the world, hunts the biggest animals on the planet.

All sharks, including the great white, are constantly on the prowl for food.

With its extreme teeth, a cookie-cutter shark feeds on a whale by ripping out a cookie-shaped piece of flesh (right).

That means whales, not nuclear submarines, are the normal diet of the cookie cutter shark. It feeds by sinking those incredible teeth into the side of the whale, and lifting out a cookie-shaped piece of flesh before the whale knows what hit it. No wonder when it comes to biting, the cookie-cutter shark really is The Most Extreme.

For More Information

Susan Evento, *Mighty Hippopotamus*. New York: Mondo, 2003.

Sally Fleming, *Ferocious Fangs*. Chanhassen, MN: Creative, 2001.

Anthony D. Fredericks, *Fearsome Fangs*. New York: Franklin Watts, 2002.

Bobbie Kalman, *Endangered Komodo Dragons*. New York: Crabtree, 2004.

Patrick Merrick, *Vampire Bats*. Chanhassen, MN: Child's World, 2001.

Heather Miller, *Mosquito*. San Diego: KidHaven Press, 2004.

Darlyne Murawski, *Spiders and Their Webs*. Washington, DC: National Geographic Society, 2004.

Elaine Pascoe, ed., *Snake-Tacular!* San Diego, Blackbirch Press, 2004.

Emily Raabe, *Vampire Bats*. New York: PowerKids Press, 2003.

Diana Thistle Tremblay, *Hippos*. San Diego: KidHaven Press, 2003.

Sally Walker, *Crocodiles*. Minneapolis: Lerner, 2004.

Glossary

anesthetic: an agent that causes loss of sensation

antidote: a remedy to counteract poison

forensic: the application of scientific knowledge to legal problems

halitosis: bad breath

hydrostone: a material that is very strong and doesn't wear

hypodermic needle: hollow needle

jaywalker: someone who crosses a street carelessly or illegally

malaria: a disease that causes chills, a high fever, and sweating

neoprene: a synthetic rubber with good resistance to oil, chemicals, and flame

proboscis: any long, flexible snout

territorial: an animal behavior that causes it to defend a certain area from others

venom: a poison produced by some animals and insects

Index